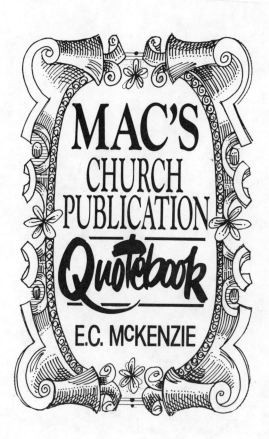

MAC'S
CHURCH
PUBLICATION
Quotebook

E.C. McKENZIE

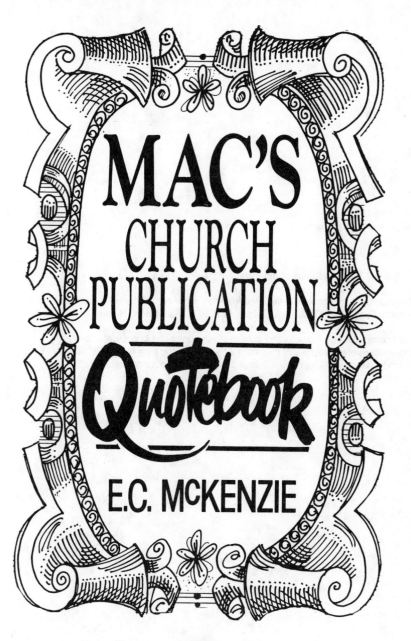

MAC'S
CHURCH
PUBLICATION
Quotebook

E.C. McKENZIE

BAKER BOOK HOUSE

Grand Rapids, Michigan 49516

Contents

Ability

We rate ability in men by what they finish, not by what they attempt.

Ability without ambition is like a car without a motor.

The remarkable thing about most of us is our ability to live beyond our means.

Ability is the most important tool in your life.

Many people doubt their ability, but few have any misgivings about their importance.

Executive ability is a talent for deciding something quickly and getting someone else to do it.

It is better to have a little ability and use it well than to have much ability and make poor use of it.

Be big enough to admit and admire the abilities of people who are better than you are.

What lies behind us and what lies before us are tiny matters compared to what lies within us.

Don't envy anybody. Every person has something no other person has. Develop that one thing and make it outstanding.

Ability will enable a man to get to the top, but it takes character to keep him there.

Personal magnetism is that indefinable something that enables us to get by without ability.

Action

Kind actions begin with kind thoughts.

People may doubt what you say, but they will always believe what you do.

We cannot do everything we want to do, but we should do everything God wants us to do.

The actions of men are the best interpreters of their thoughts.

9

God gives us the ingredients for our daily bread, but He expects us to do the baking.

Think of what others ought to be like, then start being like that yourself.

The surest way to gain respect is to earn it by conduct.

Many pious people would rather study the Bible than practice what it teaches.

Christianity requires the participants to come down out of the grandstand and onto the playing field.

The Christian's walk and talk must go together.

Your creed may be interesting, but your deeds are much more convincing.

In all relationships of life, faith is worthless unless it leads to action.

People who live by the Golden Rule today never have to apologize for their actions tomorrow.

Never judge a man's actions until you know his motives.

If you're going to climb, you've got to grab the branches, not the blossoms.

Kind words can never die, but without kind deeds they can sound mighty sick.

Where we go and what we do advertises what we are.

There's no sense aiming for a goal with no arrow in your bow.

It's not the load that breaks you down, it's the way you carry it.

Cheerfulness is contagious, but don't wait to catch it from others. Be a carrier!

The Christian who is pulling the oars doesn't have time to rock the boat.

You don't have time to criticize when you harmonize, sympathize, and evangelize.

The thing to try when all else fails is again.

The smallest good deed is better than the grandest intention.

Experience is a form of knowledge acquired in only two ways—by doing and by being done.

The true object of education should be to train one to think clearly and act rightly.

The Golden Rule is of little value unless you realize that you must make the first move.

It isn't how high you go in life that counts but how you got there.

After saying our prayers we ought to do something to make them come true.

The right angle to approach a difficult problem is the "tryangle."

The man who fails while trying to do good has more honor than he who succeeds by accident.

A spoken word and a thrown stone cannot be recalled.

Adversity

Adversity is never pleasant, but sometimes it's possible to learn lessons from it that can be learned in no other way.

All people need a faith that will not shrink when washed in the waters of affliction and adversity.

How would a person ever know whether his or her faith was weak or strong unless it has been tried and tested?

A real friend will tell you your faults and follies in times of prosperity, and assist you with his hand and heart in times of adversity.

Prosperity makes friends; adversity tries them.

God often tries us with a little to see what we would do with a lot.

Love is a fabric which never fades, no matter how often it is washed in the water of adversity and grief.

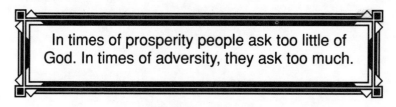

In times of prosperity people ask too little of God. In times of adversity, they ask too much.

Alcoholics

To escape alcoholism is simple. Never take the drink just before the second one.

No alcoholic is really anonymous.

An alcoholic is not one who drinks too much, but one who can't drink enough.

It is useless for alcoholics to worry about the future.

Anger

Speak when you are angry and you will make the speech you will forever regret.

Anger is a state that starts with madness and ends with regret.

When angry count ten before speaking. When very angry count one hundred and then don't speak.

For every minute you're angry, you lose sixty seconds of happiness.

Men with clenched fists cannot shake hands.

Anyone who angers you conquers you.

The world needs more warm hearts and fewer hot heads.

Form the habit of closing your mouth firmly when angry.

Be strong enough to control your anger instead of letting it control you.

Forgiveness saves the expense of anger, the high cost of hatred, and the waste of energy.

Bible

The Bible is most helpful when it is open.

Carrying a Bible will never take the place of reading it.

Many Christians expect the world to respect a book they neglect.

How can you have faith in the Bible unless you know what's in it?

We should study the Bible as a privilege, not as a duty.

Study the Bible to be wise, believe it to be safe, practice it to be holy.

Men do not reject the Bible because it contradicts itself, but because it contradicts them.

Go to your Bible regularly, open it prayerfully, read it expectantly, live it joyfully.

One of the best evidences of the inspiration and infallibility of the Bible is that it has survived the fanaticism and ignorance of its friends.

There are a number of splendid translations of the Bible. However, the most effective is its translation into the lives of people.

23

A person who merely samples the Word of God never acquires much of a taste for it.

Other books were given to us for information, but the Bible was given to us for transformation.

If you will carry the Bible while you are young, it will carry you when you are old.

The study of the Bible is a postgraduate course in the richest library of human experience.

You can't understand all you read in the Bible, but you can obey what you do understand.

The Bible finds us where we are, and with our permission, will take us where we ought to go.

Our forefathers built this country with three tools: an ax, a plow, and a book. That book was the Bible.

If the Bible is mistaken in telling us from whence we came, how can we trust it to tell us where we are going?

The knowledge, understanding, and appropriation of God's Word are the means by which a Christian grows.

Be careful how you live. You may be the only Bible some people will ever read.

No matter how many new translations of the Bible are made, people still sin the same way.

The student of truth keeps an open Bible, an open dictionary, and an open mind.

Character

Be big enough to admit and admire the abilities of people who are better than you are.

Where we go and what we do advertises what we are.

One evidence of the value of the Bible is the character of those who oppose it.

Have character—don't be one!

Character is more easily kept than recovered.

Reputation is precious, but character is priceless.

You can easily judge the character of a man by how he treats those who can do nothing for him.

To change one's character, you must begin at the control center—the heart.

One of the surest marks of good character is a person's ability to accept personal criticism without feeling malice toward the one who gives it.

Ability will enable a person to get to the top, but it takes character to keep him there.

It isn't what you have, but what you are, that makes life worthwhile.

Youth and beauty fade; character endures forever.

No one can make you feel inferior without your consent.

No man is better than his principles.

Cheerfulness

Cheerfulness is contagious, but don't wait to catch it from others. Be a carrier!

The person who gets along in the world is the one who can look cheerful and happy when he isn't.

Keep your face to the sunshine and you will never see the shadows.

Some people grow up and spread cheer, others just grow up and spread.

Child Training

Children brought up in Sunday school are seldom brought up in court.

In bringing up children it's best not to let them know it.

Training a child to follow the straight and narrow way is easy for parents—all they have to do is lead the way.

It's better to teach children the roots of labor than to hand them the fruits of yours.

Theories on how to rear children usually end with the birth of the second child.

To train children at home, it's necessary for both the children and the parents to spend some time there.

You train a child until age ten; after that you only influence him.

Train your child in the way you now know you should have gone yourself.

The best way to bring up children is never to let them down.

A mother should be like a quilt—keep the children warm but don't smother them.

Christianity

If your Christianity won't work where you are, it won't work anywhere.

If you want to convince others of the value of Christianity—live it!

An empty tomb proves Christianity; an empty church denies it.

Christianity is a way of walking as well as a way of talking.

Those who say they believe in Christianity and those who practice it are not always the same people.

Christianity requires the participants to come down out of the grandstand and onto the playing field.

Christianity has been studied and practiced for ages, but it has been studied far more than it has been practiced.

The spirit of Christianity is not to impose some kind of a creed, but to share a life.

Christianity helps us face the music, even when we don't like the tune.

Christianity, like a watch, needs to be wound regularly if it is to be kept running.

Foreign missionaries will be more successful when they can show Christianity to the heathen, and not merely tell them about it.

Too much of the Christian faith has become trimming on the dress of life instead of a part of the fabric.

Christians

A Christian must get on his knees before he can get on his feet.

To feel sorry for the needy is not the mark of a Christian—to help them is.

Christians may not see eye to eye, but they can walk arm in arm.

We are not to consider ourselves Christians simply because we think we are.

The true Christian is a person who is right-side-up in a world that is upside-down.

A Christian is one who makes it easier for other people to believe in God.

What most Christians need is fewer platitudes and better attitudes.

Two marks of a Christian: giving and forgiving.

No Christian is strong enough to carry a cross and a prejudice at the same time.

A Christian is a mind through which Christ thinks, a heart through which Christ loves, a voice through which Christ speaks, a hand through which Christ helps.

When Christians feel safe and comfortable, the church is in its greatest danger.

A Christian is a living sermon, whether or not he preaches a word.

The cross is easier to the Christian who takes it up than to the one who drags it along.

A Christian should live so that instead of being a part of the world's problems, he will be a part of the answer.

A Christian is not necessarily a man who is better than someone else, but one who is better than he would be if he were not a Christian.

No garment is more becoming to a Christian than the cloak of humility.

The knowledge, understanding, and appropriation of God's Word are the means by which a Christian grows.

Christmas

The Christmas season is only as meaningful as we make it.

Christmas carolers sing about peace on earth, but they don't tell us where.

When we throw out the Christmas tree we should be especially careful not to throw out the Christmas spirit with it.

Perhaps the best Yuletide decoration is being wreathed in smiles.

The Christmas season reminds us that a demonstration of religion is often better than a definition of it.

Keeping Christmas is good, but sharing it with others is much better.

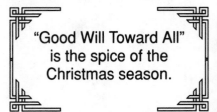 "Good Will Toward All" is the spice of the Christmas season.

The best Christmas gift of all is the presence of a happy family all wrapped up with one another.

One of the nice things about Christmas is that you can make people forget the past with a present.

Church

Separation of church and state could hardly be more complete. The church teaches that money isn't everything, and the government keeps telling us it is.

You need the church, the church needs you, the world needs both.

The collection is a church function in which many people take only a passing interest.

The church does not necessarily consist of the good, but of those who want to be better and do better.

Your faith gets a real test when you find yourself in church with nothing less than a twenty dollar bill in your wallet.

Many people give a tenth to the Lord— a tenth of what they ought to give.

Support the church with your money. You can't take it with you, but you can send it on ahead.

The surest steps toward happiness are the church steps.

The world at its worst needs the church at its best.

A place of worship should be of such character that it will be easy for men to find God and difficult for them to forget Him.

Church Attendance

Many come to church to bring their new clothes rather than themselves.

The church service is not a convention to which a family should merely send a delegate.

Many people go to church; fewer go to worship.

A man may attend church services regularly, but this does not necessarily mean he attends religiously.

Church attendance is determined more by desire than by distance.

Your willful absence from church is a vote to close its doors.

More time in God's house will bring better times in our house.

Blessed is the man whose watch keeps church time as well as business time.

Church Members

Many churches today gain more members by generation than by regeneration.

Church members are stockholders in the church, not merely spectators.

A lot of church members know the twenty-third Psalm much better than they know the Shepherd.

There are a few church members who may be described as the farmer described his mule: "Awfully backward about going forward."

Many church members have enough religion to make them decent but not enough to make them dynamic.

Common Sense

Common sense is the knack of seeing things as they are, and doing things as they ought to be done.

An unusual amount of common sense is sometimes called wisdom.

It is a thousand times better to have common sense without an education than to have an education without common sense.

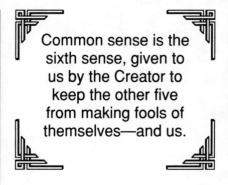

Common sense is the sixth sense, given to us by the Creator to keep the other five from making fools of themselves—and us.

It is unfortunate that common sense isn't more common.

Wisdom is nothing more than common sense refined by learning and experience.

The door to wisdom swings on hinges of common sense and uncommon thoughts.

Compliments

Don't forget that appreciation is always appreciated.

It's easy to keep from being a bore. Just praise the person to whom you are talking.

Some pay a compliment as if they expected a receipt.

It's ironic but the toughest thing to take gracefully is a compliment.

It is all right to be always looking for compliments—to give to somebody else.

There's a difference between paying compliments and paying for them.

Confession

Confessing your sins is no substitute for forsaking them.

There's more hope for a confessed sinner than a conceited saint.

Confess your sins, not your neighbor's.

Unless sin is confessed, it will fester.

Conscience

To know what is right and not do it is as bad as doing wrong.

A budget is like a conscience—it doesn't keep you from spending, but it makes you feel guilty about it.

With some people, a clear conscience is nothing more than a poor memory.

A gash in the conscience may disfigure the soul.

When a man won't listen to his conscience, it's usually because he doesn't want advice from a stranger.

A conscience is a safe guide only when God is the guide of the conscience.

One should be more concerned about what his conscience whispers than about what other people shout.

Conscience is something inside that bothers you when nothing outside does.

Conscience is not the voice of God; it is the gift of God.

It is your conscience that warns you to be careful about what it can't stop you from doing.

55

The head usher to happiness is a well-kept conscience.

Happiness is a healthy mental attitude, a grateful spirit, a clear conscience, and a heart full of love.

Conviction

Conviction is a belief that you hold or that holds you.

If you don't stand for something, you will likely fall for anything.

The difference between a prejudice and a conviction is that you can explain a conviction without getting angry.

Many convictions are family hand-me-downs.

Be bold in what you stand for, but careful in what you fall for.

If you want to convince others of the value of Christianity—live it!

Courage

The true test of moral courage is the ability to ignore an insult.

Courage is being the only one who knows you're afraid.

The courage to speak must be matched by the wisdom to listen.

Courage is something you always have until you need it.

Courage is not the absence of fear, but the conquest of it.

Courage makes both friends and foes.

Don't be afraid to go out on a limb. That's where the fruit is.

Courage is the quality it takes to look at yourself with candor, your adversaries with kindness, and your setbacks with serenity.

Freedom is the sure possession of only those who have the courage to defend it.

Keep your fears to yourself, but share your courage with others.

Courtesy

They tell us that courtesy is contagious. So why not start an epidemic?

Practice courtesy. You never know when it might become popular again.

A little of the oil of courtesy will save a lot of friction.

Courtesy costs nothing, yet it buys things that are priceless.

Why are husbands and wives more courteous to strangers than to each other?

Life is not so short that there isn't time for courtesy.

Gratitude is the most exquisite form of courtesy.

Death

The nearer the time comes for our departure from this life, the greater our regret for wasting so much of it.

Death is not a period but a comma in the story of life.

People who are afraid of death are usually afraid of life.

No one is dead as long as he is remembered by someone.

When we die we leave behind us all that we have and take with us all that we are.

There are worse things than death for some people—take life, for instance.

A single rose for the living is better than a costly wreath at the grave.

In a world where death is, we should have no time to hate.

The one thing certain about life is that we must leave it.

The only thing worse than growing old is to be denied the privilege.

Difficulties

Troubles and weeds thrive on lack of attention.

Remember the steam kettle! Though up to its neck in hot water, it continues to sing.

Tackle any difficulty at first sight, for the longer you gaze at it, the bigger it grows.

One of the most difficult mountains for people to climb is the one they make out of a molehill.

The difficulties of life are intended to make us better—not bitter.

All men need a faith that will not shrink when washed in the waters of affliction and adversity.

How would a person ever know whether his faith was weak or strong unless it has been tried and tested?

Don't make your friends a dumping ground for your troubles.

The triumphal song of life would lose its melody without its minor keys.

Have you noticed that an optimist is always able to see the bright side of other people's troubles?

A person's most fervent prayers are not said when he is on his knees, but when he is flat on his back.

He who does not pray when the sun shines will not know how to pray when the clouds come.

It's much easier to borrow trouble than to give it away.

The person who is always looking for trouble may someday discover that he's it.

Much trouble is caused by our yearnings getting ahead of our earnings.

Don't borrow trouble. Be patient and you'll soon have some of your own.

A good way to forget your troubles is to help others out of theirs.

May your troubles in the coming New Year be as short-lived as your resolutions.

God is not only a present help in time of trouble, but also a great help in keeping us out of trouble.

Trouble causes some people to go to pieces; others to come to their senses.

People always get into trouble when they think they can handle their lives without God.

Of all the troubles great or small, the greatest are those that don't happen at all.

A lot of trouble arises from workers who don't think, and from thinkers who don't work.

Worry is interest paid on trouble before it falls due.

Discipline

Character does not reach its best until it is controlled, harnessed, and disciplined.

Discipline yourself so others won't have to.

When a man praises discipline, nine times out of ten this means he is prepared to administer it rather than submit to it.

Discipline is something that can be learned during the first year of school or the first year of married life.

A really good parent is a provider, a counselor, an adviser, and when necessary, a disciplinarian.

Will power cannot be furnished by anyone but you.

Discretion

The age of discretion is when you make a fool of yourself in a more dignified way.

Discretion is simply leaving a few things unsaid.

Discretion is like a man's beard—it doesn't show up until he grows up.

Encouragement

Pat others on the back, not yourself.

The best thing to do behind a person's back is pat it.

A friend will strengthen you with his prayers, bless you with his love, and encourage you with his hope.

Keep your ideals high enough to inspire you and low enough to encourage you.

Enjoyment

Your conscience doesn't really keep you from doing anything; it merely keeps you from enjoying it.

Why not learn to enjoy the little things—there are so many of them?

Enjoy yourself. These are the "good old days" you're going to miss in the years ahead.

The good things in life were made to enjoy. Enjoying a thing means sharing it with others.

Not what we have
but what we enjoy
that constitutes our
abundance.

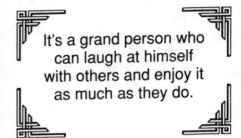
It's a grand person who
can laugh at himself
with others and enjoy it
as much as they do.

Enthusiasm

The cross is easier
to the Christian
who takes it up
than to the one
who drags it along.

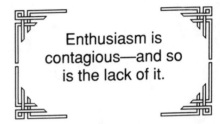
Enthusiasm is
contagious—and so
is the lack of it.

We have never learned
to support the things
we support with the
enthusiasm with which
we oppose the things
we oppose.

There's always a
good crop of food
for thought. What
we need is enough
enthusiasm to
harvest it.

He who has
no fire in
himself cannot
warm others.

Enthusiasm is the propelling
force necessary for climbing
the ladder of success.

The gap between enthusiasm and indifference is filled with failures.

Years wrinkle the skin, but lack of enthusiasm wrinkles the soul.

Envy

Some of the older generation's criticism of the younger generation is heavily tinged with envy.

A person usually criticizes the individual whom he envies.

The only person worth envying is the person who doesn't envy.

Envy is blind and knows nothing except to depreciate the excellence of others.

Don't envy anybody. Every person has something no other person has. Develop that one thing and make it outstanding.

Most of us aren't prepared to accept success—especially somebody else's.

Faith

Christianity helps us face the music, even when we don't like the tune.

Feed your faith and doubt will starve to death.

Doubt makes the mountain which faith can move.

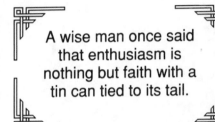

A wise man once said that enthusiasm is nothing but faith with a tin can tied to its tail.

A person's faith is not judged by what he says about it, but by what he does about it.

When you cease to use your faith, you lose it.

Faith is to the soul what a mainspring is to a watch.

The greatest act of faith takes place when a man finally decides that he is not God.

Genuine faith is assuring, insuring, and enduring.

The greatness of our fears shows us the littleness of our faith.

Faith keeps the man who keeps his faith.

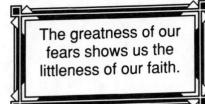
Faith gives us the courage to face the present with confidence, and the future with expectancy.

Families

The family that stays together probably only has one car.

Charity should begin at home, but most people don't stay at home long enough to begin it.

The family altar would alter many a family.

The greatest institution in the world is the human family.

Fear

When you can think of yesterday without regret and tomorrow without fear, you are near real contentment.

Courage is being the only one who knows you're afraid.

Courage is not the absence of fear, but the conquest of it.

Fear of failure is the father of failure.

The greatness of our fears shows us the littleness of our faith.

Fear falls before the fortress of faith.

The highway of fear is the shortest route to defeat.

The only thing we have to fear is not doing something about the fear we have.

Fear of the future is a waste of the present.

Forgiveness

Two marks of a Christian: giving and forgiving.

Forgiveness is a funny thing. It warms the heart and cools the sting.

Forgiveness is the perfume that the trampled flower casts upon the heel that crushed it.

It is far better to forgive and forget than to hate and remember.

Always forgive your enemies; nothing annoys them quite so much.

Forgiveness saves the expense of anger, the high cost of hatred, and the waste of energy.

Forgiveness is the key that unlocks the door of resentment and the handcuffs of hate.

It has been rightly said that forgiveness is the quality of heart that forgets the injury and forgives the offender.

Future

It's better to look where you're going than to see where you've been.

Telling children that school days are the happiest days of their lives doesn't give them much to look forward to.

Faith gives us the courage to face the present with confidence and the future with expectancy.

Fear of the future is a waste of the present.

Judging from the way things look, it's a good thing the future doesn't come all at once.

Never be afraid to trust an unknown future to a known God.

Some carve out a future, while others just whittle away the time.

The trouble with the future is that it usually arrives before we're ready for it.

It's a mistake to look too far ahead. Only one link in the chain of destiny can be handled at a time.

Most of us are still planning for the future after it is in the past.

The best thing to save for the future is your soul.

A kindness done today is the surest way to a brighter tomorrow.

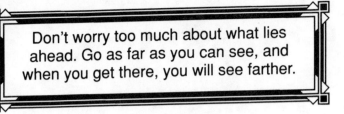

Don't worry too much about what lies ahead. Go as far as you can see, and when you get there, you will see farther.

Generosity

A lot of folks think they are generous because they give free advice.

Generosity will always leave a more pleasant memory than stinginess.

Giving until it hurts is not a true measure of generosity. Some are more easily hurt than others.

Wisdom enables one to be thrifty without being stingy, and generous without being wasteful.

Giving

Charity is twice blessed—it blesses the one who gives and the one who receives.

It is better to give than to lend, and it costs about the same.

Blessed are those who can give without remembering, and receive without forgetting.

The best thing you can give someone is a chance.

Nothing makes people more sensitive to pain than giving until it hurts.

Where there is no interest, there is no investment.

You receive in proportion and in kind as you have given.

He who gives only when he is asked has waited too long.

Give not from the top of your purse, but from the bottom of your heart.

Give your best to the world, and the best will be given back to you.

What you give lives!

God looks not to the quantity of the gift but to the quality of the giver.

You can give without loving, but you can't love without giving.

The manner of giving is worth more than the gift.

We make a living by what we get, but we make a life by what we give.

God

A person's maximum achievement often falls short of God's minimum demands.

We cannot do everything we want to do, but we should do everything God wants us to do.

God gives us the ingredients for our daily bread, but He expects us to do the baking.

When God allows a burden to be put upon you, He will put His arms underneath you to help you carry it.

A Christian is one who makes it easier for other people to believe in God.

Some people complain because God puts thorns on roses, while others praise God for putting roses among the thorns.

A conscience is a safe guide only when God is the guide of the conscience.

God never imposes a duty without giving time and strength to perform it.

It's difficult, if not impossible, to have faith in God if a person has too much faith in himself.

The greatest act of faith takes place when a man finally decides that he is not God.

Our faith deals with what God says—not what learned men say.

There are a thousand ways of pleasing God, but not one without faith.

God doesn't expect us to solve all the world's problems—He only expects us not to create them.

God cares for people through people.

God still speaks to those who take the time to listen.

The Lord calls for us to stand, though not always to understand.

Whatever God wants us to do, He will help us do it.

God often tries us with a little to see what we would do with a lot.

God has called us to play the game, not to keep the scores.

God promises a safe landing but not a calm voyage.

God doesn't call us to be successful. He calls us to be faithful.

God will never allow anything to come to you that you and He can't handle.

It may be hard to believe in God, but it's much harder not to believe in Him.

Gratitude to God should be as regular as our heartbeat.

The best way to stand up before the world is to kneel down before God.

The darkest ignorance is a person's ignorance of God.

The love of God cannot be merited or earned, but it can be spurned.

The highest knowledge is the knowledge of God.

Some people are willing to serve God, but only as His consultant.

God never tires of hearing us in prayer.

God's promises are like life preservers. They keep the soul from sinking in the sea of trouble.

The Lord didn't burden us with work. He blessed us with it.

Golden Rule

One of the troubles with the world today is that we have allowed the Golden Rule to tarnish.

Do unto others as though you were the others.

People who live by the Golden Rule today never have to apologize for their actions tomorrow.

The Golden Rule is of little value unless you realize that you must make the first move.

The Golden Rule of friendship is to listen to others as you would have them listen to you.

Goodness

The man who cannot be angry at evil usually lacks enthusiasm for good.

Between two evils, choose neither; between two goods, choose both.

4-1-97

The best way to escape evil is to pursue good.

We do more good by being good than in any other way.

There is no limit to the amount of good a man can do if he doesn't care who gets the credit.

Gratitude

There's one thing for which you should be thankful—only you and God have all the facts about yourself.

Our favorite attitude should be gratitude.

Gratitude is the rarest of all virtues, and yet we invariably expect it.

Gratitude to God should be as regular as our heartbeat.

One who receives a good turn should never forget it; one who does a good turn should never remember it.

Happiness comes when we stop wailing about the troubles we have, and offer thanks for all the troubles we don't have.

Happiness

The roots of happiness grow deepest in the soil of service.

A man has happiness in the palm of his hands if he can fill his days with real work and his nights with real rest.

The search for happiness is one of the chief sources of unhappiness.

Some pursue happiness—others create it.

Happiness is in the heart, not in the circumstances.

Basis for happiness: something to do, something to love, something to look forward to.

Happiness is getting something you wanted but didn't expect.

Happiness is not perfected until it is shared with others.

Happiness will never come to those who fail to appreciate what they already have.

Heart

It has been rightly said that forgiveness is the quality of heart that forgets the injury and forgives the offender.

Two things are bad for the heart—running upstairs and running down people.

A small gift will do if your heart is big enough.

The heart is happiest when it beats for others.

You will be happier if you will give people a bit of your heart rather than a piece of your mind.

People take heart when you give them yours.

The gospel of Jesus Christ breaks hard hearts and heals broken hearts.

The greatest reward for serving others is the satisfaction found in your own heart.

The smile that lights the face will also warm the heart.

Heaven

God promises a safe landing but not a calm voyage.

People are guided to heaven more by footprints than by guideposts.

The distance from earth to heaven is not so much a matter of altitude as it is attitude.

Heaven is a state of thankfulness for having received what we did not deserve, and for not receiving what we did deserve.

Marriages are made in heaven—so are thunder and lightning.

The main object of religion is not to get a man into heaven but to get heaven into him.

Hell

Hell will be populated by two classes of people: those who will do anything, and those who will not do anything.

Since the old-time evangelist has almost disappeared from the scene, hell doesn't seem half as hot as it used to.

You will not go to hell because you made a bad start, but because you made a bad finish.

Hell is getting out of date by today's thinking, but it is not out of business.

The man who tries to prove there is no hell usually has a personal reason for doing so.

Helpfulness

Too many people are anxious to give you advice when what you really need is help.

True charity is helping those you have every reason to believe would not help you.

Criticism should always leave a person with the feeling he has been helped.

A Christian should live so that instead of being a part of the world's problems he will be a part of the answer.

To feel sorry for the needy is not the mark of a Christian—to help them is.

When you help the fellow who's in trouble, he'll never forget you when he's in trouble again.

The best place to find a helping hand is at the end of your arm.

Honesty

An honest executive is one who shares the credit with the man who did all the work.

We should give freely and generously—and in accordance with what we reported on our income tax.

The most important person to be honest with is yourself.

There are no degrees of honesty.

Honesty gives a person strength, but not always popularity.

If you are honest only because you think it's the best policy, your honesty has already been compromised.

The practice of honesty is more convincing than the profession of holiness.

There is no acceptable substitute for honesty; there is no valid excuse for dishonesty.

Hope

Faith, hope and charity—if we had more of the first two we'd need less of the last.

Hope sees the invisible, feels the intangible, and achieves the impossible.

Hope is the anchor of the soul, the stimulus to action, and the incentive to achievement.

You can't live on hope alone, nor can you live without it.

If it were not for hope, the heart would break.

Hope is putting faith to work when doubting would be easier.

Hope is faith holding out its hand in the dark.

Human Nature

We learn some things from prosperity, but we learn many more from adversity.

An angry man is seldom reasonable; a reasonable man is seldom angry.

No matter what you do, someone always knew you would.

By nature all men are much alike, but by education they become different.

To err is human; to cover it up is even more human.

We confess small faults to convey the impression that we have no big ones.

Have you noticed that it's much easier to forgive an enemy after you get even with him?

We are like beasts when we kill. We are like men when we judge. We are like God when we forgive.

There are no great men except those who have rendered service to mankind.

It's easy to understand human nature when we bear in mind that almost everybody thinks he's an exception to most rules.

What is it about human nature that makes it easier to break a commandment than a habit?

It's easier to love humanity as a whole than to love one's neighbor.

Of all human passions, love is the strongest, for it attacks simultaneously the head, the heart, and the senses.

The weakness of man is the thing to be feared, not his strength.

A sense of values is the most important single element in human personality.

Judgment

Men of good judgment seldom rely wholly on their own.

Don't condemn the judgment of another because it differs from your own. You both may be wrong.

Your neighbor will seem like a better man when you judge him as you judge yourself.

The judgment of a man on a subject on which he is prejudiced isn't really worth much.

Justice

There's justice for all, but it doesn't seem to be equally distributed.

If a cause is just it will eventually triumph in spite of all the propaganda issued against it.

Justice is something that is too good for some people and not good enough for others.

Kindness

Friendship is a living thing that lasts only as long as it is nourished with kindness, sympathy, and understanding.

Be kind to unkind people—they need it the most.

Kindness is the ability to treat your enemy decently.

The person who sows seeds of kindness enjoys a perpetual harvest.

Kindness is the insignia of a loving heart.

Let all your words be kind, and you will always hear echoes.

The greatest thing a man can do for his heavenly Father is to be kind to His children.

The milk of human kindness never curdles.

You cannot do a kindness too soon, because you never know how soon it will be too late.

Be kind. Every person you meet is fighting a difficult battle.

The kindness you spread today will be gathered up and returned to you tomorrow.

A kindness put off until tomorrow may become only a bitter regret.

Knowledge

Heads that are filled with knowledge and wisdom have little space left for conceit.

The chief benefit of education is to discover how little we know.

Education is knowing what you want, knowing where to get it, and knowing what to do with it after you get it.

Experience is a form of knowledge acquired in only two ways—by doing and by being done.

Don't find fault with what you don't understand.

Knowledge becomes wisdom only after it has been put to practical use.

Knowledge, like lumber, is best when well seasoned.

By the time you know what it's all about, it's about over.

The best part of our knowledge is that which teaches us where knowledge leaves off and ignorance begins.

Knowing what's none of your business is just as important as knowing what is.

A little knowledge properly applied is more important than a tremendous number of facts accumulated and not utilized.

Knowledge is knowing a fact. Wisdom is knowing what to do with that fact.

Knowledge humbles great men, astonishes the common man, and puffs up the little man.

It is entirely possible to know more than you understand.

Blessed is the man who does not speak until he knows what he is talking about.

Knowledge comes by taking things apart, but wisdom comes by putting things together.

Zeal without knowledge is fanaticism.

Living

Teaching children to count is not as important as teaching them what counts.

If you want to convince others of the value of Christianity—live it!

A Christian should live so that instead of being a part of the world's problems he will be a part of the answer.

Believe that life is worth living and your belief will help create the fact.

Living without faith is like driving in a fog.

Faith helps us walk fearlessly, run confidently, and live victoriously.

Life is tragic for those who have plenty to live on and nothing to live for.

So live that your memories will be a part of your happiness.

Let's live our lives in such a way that we can laugh when we're together and smile when we're alone.

Be careful how you live. You may be the only Bible some people will ever read.

If you will live right each day, you will be neither afraid of tomorrow nor ashamed of yesterday.

What do we live for if not to make the world less difficult for each other?

People will usually take the right road when you lead them to it—not when you merely point to it.

Love

Happiness is the conviction that we are loved in spite of ourselves.

Kindness is the insignia of a loving heart.

Nothing beats love at first sight except love with insight.

Love makes a man think almost as much of a woman as he thinks of himself.

Love is sharing a part of yourself with others.

Love is an unusual game. There are either two winners or none.

The most important thing a father can do for his children is to love their mother.

Everything in the household runs smoothly when love oils the machinery.

Love is more easily demonstrated than defined.

Love is the fairest flower that blooms in God's garden.

Love does not keep a ledger of the sins and failures of others.

The train of brotherly love rides on the track of concern and compassion.

What a nice world this world would be if we loved others as we love ourselves.

Love is a fabric which never fades, no matter how often it is washed in the water of adversity and grief.

Modesty

Those who have a right to boast don't need to.

The more a man knows, the more modest he is inclined to be.

The greater the man's talent, the more becoming his modesty.

A modest man is generally admired—if people ever hear of him.

A person shouldn't be too modest. A light hidden under a bushel is seldom seen and less often appreciated.

Do all you can and make no fuss about it.

Obedience

It is our duty to obey God's commands, not to direct His counsels.

Delayed obedience is the brother of disobedience.

Every great person first learned how to obey, whom to obey, and when to obey.

Christ was one child who knew more than His parents—yet He obeyed them.

A patient cannot accept the physician and, at the same time, reject his remedy.

Patience

Patience, forbearance, and understanding are companions to contentment.

God makes a promise—faith believes it, hope anticipates it, patience quietly awaits it.

Happy homes are built with blocks of patience.

The trouble with people today is that they want to get to the promised land without going through the wilderness.

Many a man has turned and left the dock just before his ship came in.

Patience is when you listen silently to someone tell about the same operation you had.

Patience is a quality that is most needed when it is exhausted.

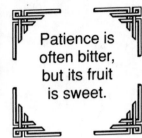
Patience is often bitter, but its fruit is sweet.

A patient man is one who can put up with himself.

Patience strengthens the spirit, sweetens the temper, stifles anger, subdues pride, and bridles the tongue.

True patience means waiting without worrying.

Peace

Peace may cost as much as war, but it's a better buy.

What the world needs is peace that passes all misunderstanding.

When a man finds no peace within himself, it is useless to seek it elsewhere.

The dove of peace still finds the world covered with the waters of hate and jealousy.

Peace is not made in documents, but in the hearts of men.

There will be no peace as long as God remains unseated at the conference table.

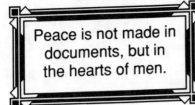 What the nations of the world need is a peace conference with the "Prince of Peace."

Peace can be achieved by the substitution of reason for force, right for might, law for war.

Perseverance

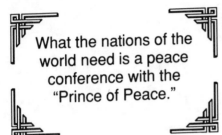 There are four steps to accomplishment: plan purposefully; prepare purposefully; prepare prayerfully; proceed positively; pursue persistently.

Just over the hill is a beautiful valley, but you must climb the hill to see it.

The man who really wants to do something finds a way; the other man finds an excuse.

If you have tried your hand at something and failed, the next best thing is to try your head.

God often tries us with a little to see what we would do with a lot.

The secret of happiness is to learn to accept the impossible, to do without the indispensable, and to bear the intolerable.

If you can think up a new idea, try finding a way to make better use of an old one.

Better the shoulder to the wheel than the back to the wall.

Any man can see farther than he can reach, but this doesn't mean he should stop reaching.

If you get up one more time than you fall, you will make it through.

Some men may succeed because they are destined to, but most men succeed because they are determined to.

To succeed— do the best you can, where you are, with what you have.

Perspective

Be big enough to admit and admire the abilities of people who are better than you are.

The greatest danger for most of us is not that our aim is too high and we miss it, but that our aim is too low and we reach it.

No one appreciates the value of constructive criticism more thoroughly than the one who's giving it.

When a man praises discipline, nine times out of ten this means he is prepared to administer it rather than submit to it.

Knowing what's none of your business is just as important as knowing what is.

We are seldom able to see an opportunity until it has ceased to be one.

If your religion leaves your life unchanged, you'd better change your religion.

Isn't it aggravating how little value other people put on your time?

Power

Men of genius are admired; men of wealth are envied; men of power are feared; but only men of character are trusted.

There is nothing in the world more powerful than an idea. No weapon can destroy it; no power can conquer it, except the power of another idea.

Knowledge is power only when it is turned on.

The greatest power for good is the power of example.

Power is dangerous unless you have humility.

Prayer provides power, poise, peace, and purpose.

This will be a better world when the power of love replaces the love of power.

Prayer

Let us pray, not for lighter burdens, but for stronger backs.

If the church is ever to get on its feet, it must get on its knees.

No one can live in doubt when he has prayed in faith.

God is never more than a prayer away.

He who would be great must be fervent in his prayers, fearless in his principles, firm in his purposes, and faithful in his promises.

Let's all bow our heads and pray as follows: "Lord, help me to admit when I am wrong, and make me easier to live with when I am right."

When life knocks you to your knees, you're in position to pray.

Prayer does not need proof, it needs practice.

If you are too busy to pray, you are too busy.

Prayer is more than asking God to run errands for us.

Don't pray for an
easy life; pray to be
a stronger person.

The secret of prayer
is prayer in secret.

The tragedy of our day is
not unanswered prayer—
but unoffered prayer.

Prayer gives
strength to the
weak, faith to
the fainthearted,
and courage to
the fearful.

Wonderful things
happen to us when
we live expectantly,
believe confidently,
and pray affirmatively.

The soul without
prayer is like
lungs without air.

Preachers

When a famous
preacher is willing
to preach in a
small church, he's
got religion.

The preacher who
cannot broaden and
deepen his sermons
usually lengthens them.

Too few preachers know the difference
between a sermon and a lecture.

The preacher's business is to preach God's will. He is an executor, not a legislator.

A preacher's audience will lose confidence in the well if every visit to the pump exhausts the water.

He who practices what he preaches may have to put in some overtime.

Perhaps you can improve your preacher's preaching by being a better listener.

He preaches well who lives well.

Some of the best preaching is done by holding the tongue.

The spirit in which a man preaches is as vital as what he says.

It takes great listening, as well as great preaching, to make a great sermon.

You can preach a better sermon with your life than with your lips.

Religion

The Christmas season reminds us that a demonstration of religion is often better than a definition of it.

People are won to your religious beliefs less by description than by demonstration.

True religion is keeping one's heart clean and hands dirty—in human service.

Religion should be the motor of life, the central heating plant of personality, the faith that gives joy to activity, hope to struggle, dignity to humility, and zest to living.

A religion that does nothing, costs nothing, suffers nothing—is worth nothing.

Some folks seem to think religion is like a parachute—something to grab when an emergency occurs.

The gospel of Jesus Christ breaks hard hearts and heals broken hearts.

Religion is not a way of looking at certain things. It is a certain way of looking at everything.

Religion furnishes education with a true sense of values. It shows what is worthwhile.

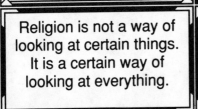

Some people think religion, like aspirin, should be taken only to relieve pain.

A religion that is small enough for us to understand would not be large enough for our needs.

The religious indifference of the masses is to be accounted for partly by the differences in the churches.

If your religion means much to you, live so it will mean much to others.

Religion doesn't fail. It's the people who fail religion.

The main object of religion is not to get a man into heaven, but to get heaven into him.

To the truly religious person, every day is Sunday.

Repentance

It takes more courage to repent than to keep on sinning.

True repentance has a double aspect. It looks upon things past with a weeping eye, and upon the future with a watchful eye.

To grieve over sin is one thing; to repent is another.

You can't repent too soon, because you don't know how soon it may be too late.

It seems that more people repent of their sins from fear of punishment than from a change of heart.

Responsibility

We increase our ability, stability, responsibility when we increase our sense of accountability to God.

We cannot do everything we want to do, but we should do everything God wants us to do.

We may not be responsible for many of the things that happen to us, but we are responsible for the way we react when they do happen.

Responsibility develops some men and ruins others.

Those who shrink from responsibilities keep on shrinking in other ways too.

Some people grow under responsibility, while others only swell.

If you would like to keep your feet on the ground, carry some responsibilities on your shoulders.

Man is responsible to God for becoming what God has made possible for him to become.

Satan

Satan is perfectly willing to have a person confess Christianity as long as he does not practice it.

For every sin Satan is ready to provide an excuse.

The only way to be good is to obey God, love your fellowman, and hate the devil.

Satan hinders prayer, but prayer also hinders Satan.

Satan is not as black as he is painted. In fact, he is more like us than we care to admit.

Satan doesn't care what we worship, as long as we don't worship God.

Self-control

He is a fool who cannot get angry, but he is a wise man who will not.

Hot words never resulted in cool judgment.

If you can pat a man on the head when you feel like bashing it in, you're a diplomat.

When a person strikes in anger, he usually misses the mark.

At no time is self-control more difficult than in time of success.

What chance can a man have to control his destiny when he can't control himself?

Self-expression is good; self-control is better.

Sermons

A Christian is a living sermon, whether or not he preaches a word.

A good example is the best sermon you can preach.

Too few preachers know the difference between a sermon and a lecture.

The sermon will be better if you listen to it as a Christian rather than a critic.

Very few people find a sermon too long if it is helpful.

It takes great listening, as well as great preaching, to make a great sermon.

The sermon you enjoy most is not likely to be the one that will do you the most good.

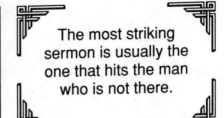

The most striking sermon is usually the one that hits the man who is not there.

Before passing judgment on a sermon, be sure to try it out in practice.

Sin

A Christian has not lost the power to sin, but the desire to sin.

A real Christian is as horrified by his own sins as he is by his neighbor's.

Confessing your sins is no substitute for forsaking them.

Love does not keep a ledger of the sins and failures of others.

There are no new sins—we just keep rerunning the old ones.

Some people seem willing to do anything to become a Christian except to give up their sins.

The three greatest sins of today are indifference to, neglect of, and disrespect for the Word of God.

Original sin is a misnomer because every kind of sin has been practiced before.

We are not punished for our sins, but by them.

You simply can't put your sins behind you until you face them.

It is the sin we try to excuse that finally gets us down.

Sincerity

Be sincere with your compliments. Most people can tell the difference between sugar and saccharine.

Prayer must mean something to us if it is to mean anything to God.

The sincere man suspects that he, too, is sometimes guilty of the faults he sees in others.

The sincerity of a person does not make false doctrine right just because he believes it.

Strength

Be strong enough to control your anger instead of letting it control you.

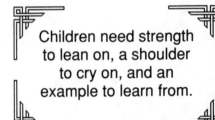

Children need strength to lean on, a shoulder to cry on, and an example to learn from.

The strength that comes from confidence can be quickly lost in conceit.

A friend will strengthen you with his prayers, bless you with his love, and encourage you with his hope.

Greatness lies not in being strong, but in the right use of strength.

Weak men wait for opportunities, strong men make them.

Prayer gives strength to the weak, faith to the fainthearted, and courage to the fearful.

Don't pray for an easy life; pray to be a stronger person.

Success

The fellow who does things that count doesn't usually stop to count them.

Our aim should be service, not success.

Ability will enable a man to get to the top, but it takes character to keep him there.

Sometimes a noble failure serves the world as faithfully as a distinguished success.

God doesn't call us to be successful. He calls us to be faithful.

Success in marriage is more than finding the right person. It's also a matter of being the right person.

The trouble with people today is that they want to get to the promised land without going through the wilderness.

Responsibility makes just as many cowards out of men as it makes successes.

At no time is self-control more difficult than in time of success.

Behind every successful person there are usually a lot of unsuccessful years.

Coming together is a beginning, keeping together is progress, working together is success.

Men sometimes credit themselves for their successes, and God for their failures.

Some men succeed by what they know, some by what they do, and a few by what they are.

If at first you don't succeed, you'll get a lot of unsolicited advice.

The man who fails while trying to do good has more honor than he who succeeds by accident.

Industry is the mother of success—luck, a distant relative.

Some men may succeed because they are destined to, but most men succeed because they are determined to.

To succeed—do the best you can, where you are, with what you have.

Wisdom is learned more from failure than from success.

Right is a bigger word than either success or failure.

Sympathy

Some folks who have a sympathetic disposition sure waste a lot of it on themselves.

A heart enlarged by sympathy has never yet killed anyone.

Sympathy is two hearts tugging at the same load.

Sympathy is the result of thinking with your heart.

The only time sympathy is ever wasted is when you give it to yourself.

One manifestation of genuine sympathy is worth more than any amount of advice.

Sympathy is the golden key that unlocks the hearts of others.

Temper

Before you give somebody a piece of your mind, be sure you can get by with what you have left.

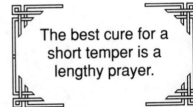
The best cure for a short temper is a lengthy prayer.

When tempers grow hot, Christianity grows cold.

A show of temper is often a testimonial of indecision, weakness, inadequacy, defeat, and frustration.

It is extremely difficult for a man who loses his temper to hold his friends.

What a wonderful thing it would be if all those who lost their tempers could find them again.

Temptation

Nothing makes it easier to resist temptation than a proper upbringing, a sound set of values, and witnesses.

Temptation seldom breaks your door down; it quietly and cunningly enters the open portals of your mind.

By yielding to temptation one may lose in a moment what it took a lifetime to gain.

Temptations from without have no power unless there is a corresponding desire within.

Temptation is something which, if resisted, may never come your way again.

Temptation is not sin, but playing with temptation invites sin.

The temptation to say an unkind word should first be rehearsed to see how it sounds to you.

Temptation can cause us to succumb, sink, sin—or stand.

Ten Commandments

God's laws last longer than those who break them.

One reason why the Ten Commandments are so short and to the point is the fact they did not come out of a committee.

A successful criminal lawyer in Montana reports that he has found several loopholes in the Ten Commandments.

The most pleasant fact about the Ten Commandments is that there are only ten of them.

Thankfulness

Thankfulness could well be the finest sentiment of man—and also the rarest.

It isn't what you have in your pocket that makes you thankful, but what you have in your heart.

Even though we can't have all we want, we ought to be thankful we don't get what we deserve.

Let us give thanks—if only for all the bad things that are never going to happen.

It is better to thank God for our achievements than to praise ourselves for them.

If you think you haven't much to be thankful for, why not be thankful for some of the things you don't have?

Tongue

The Christian should learn two things about his tongue—how to hold it and how to use it.

Good deeds speak for themselves. The tongue only interprets their eloquence.

It has been said that dignity is the ability to hold back from the tongue that which never should have been on the mind in the first place.

Speaking in tongues sometimes prevents us from telling the truth.

Happiness is often punctured by a sharp tongue.

Some of the best preaching is done by holding the tongue.

People who can hold their tongues rarely have any trouble holding their friends.

When people hold their tongues you can't tell a fool from a sage.

Truth

When in doubt, tell the truth.

Blessed are our enemies, for they tell us the truth when our friends flatter us.

It is one thing to show a man he is in error, and quite another to put him in possession of the truth.

There is not true greatness where simplicity, goodness, and truth are absent.

People cannot, or will not, learn truths which are too complicated, and they forget truths which are too simple.

The truth may hurt, but a lie is agony.

Truth is often violated by falsehood, but can be equally outraged by silence.

Truth is so precious, some people use it sparingly.

The truth is one thing for which there are no known substitutes.

Beware of the half-truth. You might get hold of the wrong half.

As scarce as the truth is, the supply has always been in excess of the demand.

Few people seek to discover truth; most of us seek to confirm our errors and perpetuate our prejudices.

Values

It is extremely easy for us to give our major attention to minor matters.

Money can build a house, but it takes love to make it a home.

The things in life that count most are the things that can't be counted.

In your search for riches, don't lose the things that money can't buy.

The relative value of health and wealth depends on which you have left.

The highest values are priceless.

Most folks pay too much for the things they get for nothing.

The value of all things, even our lives, depends on the use we make of them.

We rearrange our furniture, our flowers, and our finances—but how about our values?

The things of greatest value in life are those things that multiply when divided.

A sense of values is the most important single element in human personality.

It is what we value, not what we have, that makes us rich.

Virtue

Maybe we were better off when charity was a virtue instead of a deduction.

Sometimes we learn more from a man's errors than from his virtues.

Gratitude is the rarest of all virtues, and yet we invariably expect it.

Sometimes virtue and prosperity have trouble living together.

To know what not to think about is a major intellectual virtue.

Man's greatest vices are the misuses of his virtues.

When one robs another of virtue, he loses his own.

While virtue is its own reward, most people are looking for a better offer.

Virtue has more admirers than followers.

He who parades his virtues seldom leads the parade.

Vision

It's better to look where you're going than to see where you've been.

Faith is the daring of the soul to go farther than it can see.

Few people have sight good enough to see their own faults.

The world might be improved with less television and more vision.

We usually see things, not as they are, but as we are.

Man is like a tack; he can go only as far as his head will let him.

Any man can see farther than he can reach, but this doesn't mean he should quit reaching.

The world would be happier if its leaders had more vision and fewer nightmares.

Wealth

A person's character is put to a severe test when he suddenly acquires or quickly loses a considerable amount of money.

It is not by a man's purse, but by his character, that he is rich or poor.

The two great tests of character are wealth and poverty.

Men of genius are admired; men of wealth are envied; men of power are feared; but only men of character are trusted.

The greatest wealth is contentment with a little.

Our Lord is needed on the avenue as much as in the alley.

A man never gets so rich that he can afford to lose a friend.

A lot of people lose their health trying to become wealthy, and then lose their wealth trying to get back their health.

It's pretty hard to tell what brings happiness; poverty and wealth have both failed.

The relative values of health and wealth depend on which you have left.

The real measure of a man's wealth is how much he would be worth if he lost all his money.

The kind of wealth most of us need isn't dollars as much as sense.

Wisdom

To profit from good advice requires more wisdom than to give it.

Advice is that which the wise don't need and fools won't take.

Years make all of us old and very few of us wise.

Age doesn't always bring wisdom. Sometimes age comes alone.

He is a fool who cannot get angry, but he is a wise man who will not.

An unusual amount of common sense is sometimes called wisdom.

The courage to speak must be matched by the wisdom to listen.

You can buy education, but wisdom is a gift from God.

Experience increases our wisdom but doesn't seem to reduce our follies.

A wise man can sometimes learn from a fool—as soon as it can be determined which is which.

Wise is the man who fortifies his life with friendships.

Knowledge becomes wisdom only after it has been put to practical use.

Knowledge is like dynamite—dangerous unless handled wisely.

Knowledge comes by taking things apart, but wisdom comes by putting things together.

It is always wise to put off until tomorrow what we ought not to do at all.

To be thought wise, keep your mouth shut.

One can easily recognize a wise man by the things he doesn't say.

Our wisdom usually comes from our experience, and our experience comes largely from our foolishness.

You can't pay cash for wisdom. It comes to you on the installment plan.

Wisdom is the right use of knowledge.

It is wise to act wise, unless you're otherwise.

As a man grows older and wiser, he talks less and says more.

The word that is sufficient to the wise is usually enough for the rest of us, too.

Words

Some people can talk Christianity by the yard, but they can't, or won't, walk it by the inch.

The Christian's walk and talk must go together.

Let all your words be kind, and you will always hear kind echoes.

Learn to speak kind words—nobody resents them.

Never part without loving words. They might be your last.

The man who has to eat his own words never asks for another serving.

Kind words do not wear out the tongue—so speak them.

The three most difficult words to speak are: "I was mistaken."

A spoken word and a thrown stone cannot be retrieved.

Another form of wastefulness is the expenditure of words beyond the income of ideas.

One thing you can give and still keep is your word.

Those who have the most to say usually say it with the fewest words.

Our words may hide our thoughts, but our actions will reveal them.

Words should be used as tools of communication and not as a substitute for action.

When you break your word, you break something that cannot be mended.

Work

Just over the hill is a beautiful valley, but you must climb the hill to see it.

Ambition never gets anywhere until it forms a partnership with work.

Christianity is a roll-up-your-sleeves religion.

Christianity, like a watch, needs to be wound regularly if it is to be kept running.

What the church needs today is more calloused hands and fewer calloused hearts.

If you burn the candle at both ends you are not as bright as you think.

Families that pray together stay together; and families that work together—eat.

To love and to labor is the sum of life; and yet, how many think they are living when they neither love nor labor?

Most of us pray for more things than we are willing to work for.

A successful man continues to look for work after he has found a job.

You won't find many rules for success that will work unless you do.

It will be a great day when everybody who has a job is working.

World

You need the church, the church needs you, and the world needs both.

Friendship is the only cement that will hold the world together.

By improving yourself, the world is made better.

How different the world would be if we did as well today as we expect to do tomorrow.

The biggest problem in the world could have been settled when it was small.

We can only change the world by changing people.

If we wish to make a new world, we have the material ready. The first one was also made out of chaos.

The world owes you a living, but only when you have earned it.

The world we live in is old-fashioned. It still judges a man by what he does.

Give the world what it needs and it will supply yours.

A bitter world cannot be sweetened by a sour religion.

This will be a better world when the power of love replaces the love of power.

Worship

If God is small enough for us to understand, He isn't big enough for us to worship.

Too many try to get something from worship without putting anything into it.

Most folks seem to want the right to worship, and to make others worship the same way.

If we are going to fight for the liberty to worship, we ought to make use of that liberty.

A place of worship should be of such character that it will be easy for men to find God and difficult for them to forget Him.

To truly worship God is to carry the spirit of worship into every facet of our lives.

We can only worship God when we have prepared ourselves to be in His presence, and want to know Him.

We sometimes worship what we have achieved, rather than praising God for giving us the means of achieving it.

Zeal

The cross is easier for the Christian who takes it up than for the one who drags it along.

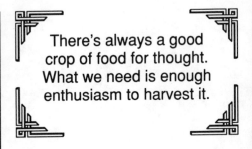
There's always a good crop of food for thought. What we need is enough enthusiasm to harvest it.

He who has no fire in himself cannot warm others.

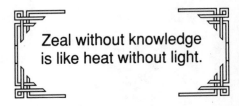
Zeal without knowledge is like heat without light.

There is no zeal so intemperate and cruel as that which is backed by ignorance.

Zeal without knowledge is the sister of folly.

If people were more zealous and less jealous, this world would be a much better place in which to live.